5+5 FNPhenomenal Ways to Save $100 This Week Without Killing Your Lifestyle

A Modern Girl's Guide to Being Phenomenal + Financially Free

BY AISHA TAYLOR

Dedicated to Mommy, Daddy, Rhiana, Liana, and Grandma. I love you.

~

ACKNOWLEDGEMENTS

First, I want to thank God, the rock from which I draw my strength and my purpose. With God, all things are possible.

Second, I want to thank my family—my parents, my two sisters, and my grandma—for their unwavering support and unconditional love.

Third, I would like to thank Eric for being my pebble, always there for me through thick and thin (including editing, proofreading, and brainstorming).

Fourth, thank you to Theresa, Dana, and Create Space for editing my book. Also, thank you to Lori (LoriEvelyn.com) for illustrating. I really appreciate you!

Fifth, thank you to anyone I didn't specifically mention. I cannot possibly list everyone, but I love you all for keeping in touch through social media, helping me as I needed it, giving me a call to encourage me, or offering your well wishes. Your constant support does not go unnoticed, and I appreciate you.

Finally, thank you to the readers who have entrusted me to help you make this FNPhenomenal journey. I truly appreciate you and am excited to serve you.

CONTENTS

" YOU CAN BE FRUGAL AND PHENOMENAL.

- AISHA TAYLOR

"

ABOUT AISHA

Aisha Taylor is a financial freedom expert who brings a modern and fresh twist to wealth consciousness.

She lives in Detroit, Michigan, with her extensive shoe collection and loves to travel, spend time with family and friends, serve the community, and escape for quiet reflection by watching boats sail by on the Detroit River. She often reminds herself that although she may not be where she wants to be, she's thankful for the bumps in the road and is grateful for the progress she has made.

Aisha holds bachelor's degrees in public policy and economics from Duke University and master's degrees in business administration and health services administration from the University of Michigan. Aisha also completed the Certified Financial Planning® program and passed the licensing exam. She currently works as a senior financial analyst for a Fortune 100 company.

Although Aisha had been well instructed in how to manage money, she fell into the trap of "keeping up with the Joneses" and had to develop a positive relationship with money in order to reach financial freedom. After graduating from business school, she, with the help of her father, created a plan that allowed her to repay student loan debt and eliminate credit debt while still sustaining a high quality of life. Aisha's true passion, however, lies in making a significant impact on the world community through volunteerism.

By founding Frugal-n-Phenomenal (FNPhenomenal), Aisha is continuing on the road toward self-improvement through pursuing knowledge, helping to build her community, and utilizing her resources to educate others. The mission of FNPhenomenal is to help women break the vicious cycle of making money but not keeping it, and to help women live frugally yet phenomenally. This is accomplished by helping them to feel worthy enough to keep their money, changing their mind-set, providing education about money management, encouraging them to live their authentic selves, and by pursuing what makes them phenomenal.

To learn more about FNPhenomenal and to inquire about working with Aisha, visit her website at www.FNPhenomenal.com or email her at aishataylor@fnphenomenal.com.

INTRODUCTION

I loved to watch *Sex and the City*. I loved to read *Glamour* magazine. And as a broke undergrad and grad school student, I imagined what it would be like to have money once I graduated and got a job. This life I created consisted of having a superpimpin' closet, fabulous shoes, a new outfit for every party, and a schedule full of hot events and endless happy hours with friends. In my head, I was living out the fantasy of so many *Modern Girls*: independent, educated women with phenomenal careers who have a buzzing social life. Eventually, I did live that life. However, it wasn't compatible with my financial situation.

I lived the life I thought I was supposed to live, not the life I could afford. I rationalized my spending even when I didn't have the money, and ultimately I fell into the endless trap of charging my clothes, my shoes, and my fun to my favorite pink credit card. I had no control, and I was too proud to share my financial woes with others. Even when I knew I was overextending myself, I was too ashamed to ask if we could do something less expensive, or pass on the shopping trip.

I had to get control of my finances if I ever wanted to get off the proverbial financial treadmill—paying down credit card debt and charging those cards back up—and have the financial freedom and life I desired. However, in order to stick to my plan, I needed something simple that wouldn't cramp my lifestyle.

I decided to write this guide because I know I'm not alone in making poor financial decisions in order to "fit in." I want to let women facing similar challenges know that living within your means can be just as sexy and, in fact, downright FNPhenomenal. I hope that this guide empowers you to start thinking differently about money and to make small changes in your life that will eventually have a large impact. The tips I share in this guide are straightforward, low-effort options that I learned to help me save money without killing my lifestyle.

This guide follows the lives of four women: Nina, Bretta, Jordan, and Amber. Just as these women examined their own lives to identify money-saving strategies to fit their needs, you too will need to examine the areas in your own life to which you can apply the appropriate money-saving strategies. Use the FNPhenomenal Action Items, Questions as You Develop Your Strategy, and the Reflection Page at the end of each chapter to examine the "why" behind your spending habits, and write down ideas to implement the

do-it-yourself solutions in this guide.

My hope is that you'll learn from the stories of Nina, Bretta, Jordan, and Amber, leverage their experiences, engage in quiet reflection, and then apply these lessons to your own life. Use this guide as a support system, and grab some friends to take the journey with you. This guide will help you continue to enjoy what makes you happy—only now you'll be doing it the FNPhenomenal way.

> **I lived a life I thought I was supposed to live, not the life I could actually afford.**

NINA

TIP 01:
TACKLING THE "LETS DO LUNCH" EXPENSE

Nina is a twenty-eight-year-old advertising account executive who lives in Chicago. She works in a modern office building with a nice food court and tons of cute restaurants nearby. Nina works about fifty-five hours a week. One thing she does faithfully is go to lunch with her coworker Bretta (age twenty-seven) and her best friend, Amber (age twenty-eight), who also works in the building. When they go out to lunch, they catch up on daily gossip, television, and the events they plan to attend.

One day Nina came across an article that discussed Costa Rica as an amazing vacation destination. She was immediately interested and told Bretta and Amber about the potential vacation at lunch the next day. Bretta and Amber were instantly on board with the idea and wanted to start planning the trip.

Given that it was her idea, Nina felt compelled to go on the trip, but given her financial constraints, she realized it could be a problem. The five-day, four-night trip would cost her about $2,000 total, and she didn't have that kind of money. Even though Nina made about $70,000 a year, she had no clue where her money went. She decided that she needed to take some steps to identify how to save the necessary money, because she *refused* to miss this trip.

Nina signed up for Mint.com, a personal financial management service, and found, to her surprise, that she was spending $2,250

per year on lunch! It turned out that her weekly dates with Amber and Bretta cost her $45 a week, and she worked fifty weeks per year. This was actually on the higher end, because the annual cost of purchased lunches in 2012 in the United States, according to the recruiting agency Accounting Principals, was $2,000. By spending $2,250 per year, Nina was a bit higher than the national average.

Nina was shocked. She couldn't believe that those eight- to ten-dollar meals added up to that amount. She'd never considered looking at her annual lunch expense. Armed with this information, Nina told Bretta and Amber that she needed their support to help her make some financial improvements. Nina asked them if they would be open to bringing their lunch four out of five days a week, or at least eating in the food court more often, so that Nina could bring a homemade lunch but still eat with her friends. Nina settled on four days a week because she knew that going from never bringing her lunch to bringing it five days per week just wasn't realistic. However, even making the change to four days would save her $1,800 a year.

> **Look at your annual lunch expenses. Those eight-to-ten-dollar meals add up.**

Nina was surprised to learn that Bretta and Amber were also trying to figure out how they would save the money for the trip. They agreed to Nina's plan for eating lunch. When they thought about why they always bought lunch, they realized none of them ever felt like making a lunch because it seemed hard, time-consuming, and something that older people with kids did.

To combat this, they decided to make bringing lunch fun by experimenting with different ideas and changing the locations where they ate lunch to include outdoor parks and other buildings. On Fridays, they were allowed to go to a restaurant; however, they set a strict budget of ten dollars, including a tip.

They also developed these "protections" to ensure that they adhered to the plan:

- Make lunch for the week on Sunday.
- Cook in bulk in order to leverage the items for lunch and dinner.
- Portion all the prepared food so that it's easy to "grab and go."
- Text each other on Sunday evening as an accountability check-in.

Nina was ecstatic to have a plan and to assist her friends with their saving goals in the process! With $1,800 down, she only had to find $200 more.

FNPhenomenal Action Item

1. Sign up for Mint.com to understand where your money is going.
2. Identify the number of times you "do lunch" per week, and think about why you go.
3. If your reasons are social, speak to your friends and coworkers. They may want to be your partners in being Frugal-n-Phenomenal.
4. Identify your lunch strategy.
5. Find friends who can hold you accountable in achieving your goals.

Questions to Ask as You Identify Your Lunch Strategy

1. What can I bring to lunch that is simple, tasty, and easy to prepare?
2. Can I eat the same thing every day, or learn to do so? If not, how can I add variety without creating a burden?
3. How can I shop for groceries to ensure that my refrigerator is properly stocked?
4. What can I do to ensure that my plan is easy to adhere to?
5. What about Nina do I most identify with?

Potential Weekly Savings

Potential Weekly Savings: $25 (assuming $7 per day lunch purchase versus $2 per day brown-bag lunch for 5 days)

Amount Saved per Week: _____

Annual Savings: _____ x 4 x 12 = _____

JORDAN

TIP 02:
TRANSFORMING THE TAKEOUT QUEEN

Jordan is a twenty-six-year-old marketing professional who's always on the move. She's always attending an event or involved in a community service project. And she works sixty hours a week because she wants to make that next promotion. Jordan is busy with a capital *B*! It's hard to catch up with her. In fact, although she wanted to go on the girls' trip to Costa Rica, not surprisingly she couldn't fit it into her hectic schedule.

Jordan has it all together from the social and professional perspectives, but when it comes to her finances, not so much. She earns a fairly high salary, but with her student loan payments and other expenses, sometimes she feels like she's just getting by. Even if she had the time to go to Costa Rica, she wouldn't have been able to afford the trip. Tired of living paycheck to paycheck, she finally thought, "Enough is enough!" and decided to start making some changes.

Having a great career and community reputation does not necessarily translate into being financially sound. We all need to work on something!

As Jordan sat down to figure out where her money was going, she thought about the fact that she orders takeout food almost every night for dinner. Each time she buys food, she spends about fifteen dollars per meal. That's at least $105 each week ($420 per month and $5,000 per year) on dinner alone. Jordan does not like to prepare dinner after her long days, and it's really easy to make an excuse to grab that convenient takeout menu. But as she thought about her student loan debt and her desire to start an investment account, she quickly realized that although she loves convenience, she doesn't love it *that* much!

Although Jordan knew that she needed to make some changes, time was still a factor. (Also, she needed to stop using her oven as an "extra closet," à la Carrie in *Sex and the City*.) She approached the time-versus-money trade-off in the following manner:

• She calculated how much time picking up takeout *really* took, including the drive to and from the restaurant. Once she timed the process, she noticed that the restaurant wasn't actually on her way home. The restaurant was in the same general direction, but Jordan didn't *have* to pass by it to get home, so she was actually *adding* time to her commute—not to mention the additional gas expense.

• She considered the time it took to wait in line at the restaurant, and the time for the order to be cooked. Even when she called in the order ahead of time, sometimes it wasn't ready when she arrived at the restaurant.

- She concluded that she could make dinner at home, saving both money and time.

Jordan needed convenience in order to stick to the plan and avoid the "Ah! I forgot to go to the grocery store!" moments, so she decided to keep a few staples in the house at all times. By purchasing items in bulk from a warehouse club such as Costco, on sale at a grocery store, or at a farmers' market, she now has food on hand that she can cook quickly in order to have dinner ready within ten to fifteen minutes, which is shorter than the time to pick up takeout and get home. These bulk items include frozen shrimp, frozen fish (individually vacuum sealed), frozen broccoli, a two-pound bag of spinach, and rice (no more than four to six pounds). Sometimes Jordan makes the rice at the beginning of the week so she can quickly make a fried rice dish or rice and beans during the week. To avoid boredom and ensure that she doesn't waste food, she uses websites such as Super Cook (www.supercook.com) and My Fridge Food (myfridgefood.com) to cook meals using items she already has in her kitchen. These sites make it easy to know which ingredients are missing so they can be added to a shopping list or dug out of the back of a spice cabinet.

Once Jordan understood the time-versus-money trade-off and how to stock her kitchen in a manner that makes cooking easy, she decided to cook dinner four to five days per week. Given her schedule, she also wanted to understand how to maximize the time spent cooking. Since weekends offered her more flexibility, she decided to cook on Sunday and portion her dinners for the entire workweek. For those meals, she targeted an average dinner price of three dollars per meal rather than the fifteen dollars per meal that she had been spending. This saved $48 (four days) to $60 (five days) per week. Over the course of the year, this resulted in savings between $2,500 (four days) and $3,100 (five days). Jordan decided to put half of these savings into repaying student loans, and the other half into an investment account.

Although she developed a solid plan to reduce her consumption of takeout, Jordan knew that on some days getting takeout would be inevitable. On those days, she ordered a portion large enough for two meals—the current day's dinner and lunch or dinner for the next day—and thus cut the cost of the dinner in half.

From a financial perspective, cooking instead of buying takeout just makes sense—and cents!

FNPhenomenal Action Item

1. Identify staple food items you can keep in your pantry or freezer that will eliminate excuses for not cooking.
2. Pick a strategy: cooking for the week on a Sunday (or another day that is convenient), or cooking periodically throughout the week.
3. Start!

Questions to Ask as You Identify Your Takeout Strategy

1. Which foods and recipes can be used quickly to develop a dinner menu that lasts for a few days?
2. Which day do I have the most free time to cook in bulk?
3. What are the best times and days to shop for groceries?
4. How often will I shop?
5. How can I structure my days to minimize the need to get takeout?
6. If I have a busy day scheduled, how can I strategize to bring my meals with me for the entire day?
7. What about Jordan do I most identify with?

Potential Weekly Savings

Potential Weekly Savings: $60 (assuming $15 takeout dinner versus $3 home-cooked dinner for 5 days)

Amount Saved per Week: _____
Annual Savings: _____ x 4 x 12 = _____

REFLECTION PAGE

BRETTA

TIP 03:
MANAGING THE HAPPY-HOUR EXPENSE

Bretta, Nina's coworker, is a twenty-seven-year-old social media strategist. Bretta just loves being out and about and on the scene, and she never turns down an invitation to go to happy hour. She can be found at happy hour on Mondays, Wednesdays, and—of course—Fridays, which gets expensive. Even paying happy-hour prices, she easily spends thirty dollars a night. In addition to the lunch savings that Nina suggested, Bretta still needs to save about $200 so that she can go to Costa Rica. However, as she looked at how she spent her money, she understood that she needed to make larger changes than just the Costa Rica savings. Bretta has about $15,000 in credit card debt. This debt is on a card she predominately uses to fund her socialite lifestyle.

As she thought about why she was always going out, she asked herself the following questions: What is it that I enjoy so much about going to happy hour? Am I going to happy hour because the places are cool and trendy? Am I going to spend quality time with friends?

She knew that she loved to spend time with her friends, so she suggested that they move the Wednesday happy hour to Thursday and have *Scandal*-watching parties on Thursdays. They could rotate the party among her friends' homes, where they could get a few bottles of wine (no more than ten dollars per bottle) and light snacks (e.g., popcorn, chips, and dip) for

a total of fifty dollars. One of Bretta's friends suggested that they try economical wine (i.e., four dollars a bottle) to drive their date nights down to thirty dollars. On Bretta's off-weeks to host, this strategy saved her thirty dollars a week. This was phenomenal because she got the same great friendship and company at a fraction of the price!

However, Bretta also loved the scene. As she reflected, she recognized that some of her happy-hour attendance was because she loved to see people, and she loved to be seen. She was making $50,000 a year, but she lived like she made a lot more. She asked herself, "Who is paying my bills? Is being on the scene worth the financial sacrifice? Who is Bretta and what does she like and want to do?"

She also started to wonder what else she could be doing. Was there something she was passionate about that she could be working on, instead of spending her time after work at the restaurant or the bar? Could she participate in service projects or start her own business? Going through this process was difficult because it forced Bretta to assess whether she truly enjoyed the things and people to which she had grown accustomed. She was also forced to compare what she had been doing to what she *could* be doing. Although this self-reflection was difficult, the outcome made it a productive use of her time.

Bretta decided to eliminate the Monday happy hour and use that time to explore other areas she was interested in. This saved her thirty dollars a week.

She started to volunteer as an after-school tutor to help improve reading comprehension for young girls. This activity not only fulfilled Bretta mentally and emotionally, but also spiritually. Yes, she saved money, but as time passed, saving money became secondary. She was glad to use her talent to help change lives.

After a month and a half of saving between thirty and sixty dollars per week, Bretta saved more than enough money for the balance of the Costa Rica trip. She also donated 30 percent of her savings to the local nonprofit where she volunteered, and she put the remaining 70 percent toward her credit card debt repayment. Most importantly, Bretta started to understand and truly love who she was as a person.

FNPhenomenal Action Item

1. Think about why you are going to happy hour. Is it the time with friends, being seen, or something else?
2. Propose limiting happy hour at a restaurant or bar to once a week, and ask your friends to participate in a rotating happy-hour gathering at each of your homes.
3. Identify where you will put the savings from this category.

Questions to Ask as You Identify Your Happy-Hour Strategy

1. Why am I going to happy hour regularly?
2. Am I going in order to spend quality time with my friends, or am I going just to be seen?
3. Is this something I enjoy, or something I feel I have to do?
4. Can my friends and I come up with a way to spend time with one another that saves money?
5. Is there something I've wanted to try but never made the time to (e.g., serving the community, visiting a museum, or spending time with family)? Can I do that activity instead?
6. Is my social calendar stopping me from making gains in my financial health or other aspects of my life?
7. What about Bretta do I most identify with?

Potential Weekly Savings

Potential Weekly Savings: $30–$60

Amount Saved per Week: _____
Annual Savings: _____ x 4 x 12 = _____

AMBER

TIP 04:
BUY YOUR WATER IN BULK

Amber is a twenty-eight-year-old public relations professional. She loves drinking water because it is great for the skin and good for the body. Even when she's on the run, which she is most of the time, she always drinks at least the recommended nine cups daily—almost five bottles of water per day. When she runs out, she stops at a gas station or convenience store to buy a bottle for $1.39.

While thinking about where she would find the rest of the money to save for her trip to Costa Rica, Amber examined her spending on bottled water. As she thought about this more, she came up with a few options to reduce the cost:

Option 1: She could buy bottled water from a bulk retailer at $3.49 per case of thirty-five, which is about ten cents per bottle. This would save her about forty-five dollars per week, assuming that she drinks five bottles of water per day.

Option 2: Instead of keeping five plastic bottles with her each day, she can carry one and implement a refill strategy: when the bottle is empty, she can fill it with filtered tap water. This would require bringing only one bottle of water to work and refilling it throughout the day. This would save her about forty-eight dollars per week, again assuming that she drinks five bottles of water per day and buys in bulk.

Option 3: Instead of buying cases of plastic

> **Use a refill strategy: Buy only one bottle of water, and when the bottle is empty, refill it with filtered tap water.**

water bottles, Amber can "go green" and buy a single BPA-free bottle for less than twenty dollars. As with the plastic bottle in Option 2, she can carry and refill this bottle with filtered water. After the initial investment in the water bottle, Amber's ongoing savings would be forty-nine dollars per week.

Amber decided on a combination of Options 1 and 2. During the workweek, she would use Option 2 and just refill her water bottle. On weekends, assuming it wasn't too hot outside, she would leave the other bottles in the car to avoid having to purchase a bottle while she was out. This way she could avoid the inconvenience of carrying around several water bottles. The only reason she didn't choose Option 3 was that she was concerned about washing the bottle frequently and carrying it around when it was empty.

Amber knew that she needed to be more disciplined in her planning, and she often reminded herself of a quote by Benjamin Franklin: "By failing to prepare, you are preparing to fail." By planning, Amber could save $2,300 per year. She could put $200 toward the Costa Rica trip and use the remainder to start a "just-in-case account" for expenses that pop up throughout the year, such as car repairs and home repair. The just-in-case account would help her to stop charging these unplanned expenses to her credit card.

> "By failing to prepare, you are preparing to fail."
> - Benjamin Franklin

FNPhenomenal Action Item

1. Get a membership to a bulk retailer. If two cards come with a membership, find a friend to split the cost with you.
2. Buy cases of water from the bulk retailer.
3. Estimate how many bottles you need to carry with you throughout the day, or learn where you can refill a bottle that you bring.

Questions to Ask as You Identify Your Bottled-Water Strategy

1. Which option will I choose?
2. How will I prepare to ensure that I minimize the risk of buying water throughout the day?
3. What will be my trigger to purchase the next case of water?
4. If I choose Option 1 or 2, where will I buy my water? If it isn't a bulk retailer, how will I ensure that I am not paying more than ten cents per bottle?
5. What about Amber do I most identify with?

Potential Weekly Savings

Potential Weekly Savings: $45 (assuming $1.39 per bottle and 5 bottles per day)

Amount Saved per Week: _____

Annual Savings: _____ x 4 x 12 = _____

REFLECTION PAGE

TIP 05:
THE SUPERPIMPIN' LATTE SWAP

Given that Nina was $200 away from her goal to save $2,000 for the trip to Costa Rica, she needed to find another way to save.

Nina knew that saving money by bringing her lunch would take some preparation, so she wanted her second change to be smaller—something that required a minimal time commitment. As she started to think, she remembered her obsession with Starbucks: she goes to Starbucks five or six times per week and always orders a skinny vanilla latte. As Nina started to examine her finances more closely, she noticed that each skinny vanilla latte cost between four and five dollars. Since she loves the taste and the routine of stopping at Starbucks almost daily, instead of totally cutting that routine out of her day, she made

a "smart swap" and started getting a regular coffee with vanilla syrup and a splash of skim milk. Same taste, but her wallet stays plump!

This swap allowed her to continue to enjoy a store that she loves and still save money. Switching to coffee saves Nina $1.60 per day. Considering that she goes to Starbucks between five and six times per week, this change will save her between $415 and $500 a year. In Nina's case, that's enough to pay for the remainder of the Costa Rica trip and have enough left over to start an emergency savings account. That probably doesn't sound like much, but it's better than zero. The best part is that she gets to keep her trips to Starbucks, which are clearly crucial to starting her day off right!

"A change that allows you to tweak one aspect of a routine without eliminating or changing the experience."

FNPhenomenal Action Item

1. Identify a favorite coffee drink you can modify to make it more cost-effective.
2. Play with the proportions of milk and sweetener until they are just right. This may take a few tries.

Questions to Ask as You

Identify Your Coffee Strategy

1. What beverage can I modify to make it more cost-effective?
2. Do I have to buy coffee every day?
3. In Tip 2, Jordan discovered that her takeout place wasn't exactly on the way home. Is there a coffee place on the way or closer that I can switch to?
4. What else can I do or order to save money?
5. What about Nina do I most identify with?

Potential Weekly Savings

Potential Weekly Savings: $8 (assuming 5 visits per week)

Amount Saved per Week: _____
Annual Savings: _____ x 4 x 12 = _____

PLUS 01:
THE WEEKLY MANICURE

After Jordan started to make changes to her takeout routine, she thought to herself, "I know I can do more." She wanted to create a savings account to give her breathing room and to reduce the stress of living paycheck to paycheck.

Jordan thought about her weekly manicure. She loves having nice nails and getting pampered. However, as she reevaluated her spending, she questioned whether the weekly manicure was necessary. Besides, with her schedule it took effort to squeeze in that time to get her nails done. Jordan thought about her options: she could get a polish change instead of a full manicure, or she could polish her own nails.

Either way, she would move from weekly to monthly manicures. Having no idea how to paint her own nails, Jordan initially started just getting polish changes for five dollars. A few times when she couldn't get to the salon, she experimented with filing and shaping her own nails and going without the polish. That do-it-yourself solution started to save her forty-five dollars a month.

As she got used to this change, she became brave enough to learn how to paint her own nails by watching a YouTube video. Now she paints her nails during the commercials of her favorite television shows. Great use of time, and it saves money!

FNPhenomenal Action Item

1. Evaluate how often you really need to get a manicure/pedicure. Are you going because you need to go, or are you going out of habit?
2. Try to stretch the time between visits to the nail salon. Can you add in an extra week? After you add in the week, how about two?
3. Try to avoid migrating to CND Shellac or gel polish when you stretch the week. CND Shellac and gel polish are more expensive, so you aren't saving much money even if you are visiting the nail salon less frequently.

Questions to Ask as You
Identify Your Manicure
Strategy

1. Am I going to go to the salon less frequently?
2. Will I switch to just polish changes?
3. If I go to the salon less frequently, what will I do with the extra time?
4. Can I apply this strategy to pedicures to save more money? Can I stretch the time between pedicures?
5. What about Jordan do I most identify with?

Potential Weekly Savings

Potential Weekly Savings: $11

Amount Saved per Week: _____
Annual Savings: _____ x 4 x 12 = _____

REFLECTION PAGE

PLUS 02:
OVERCOMING THE FEAR OF BEING CAUGHT ON SOCIAL MEDIA

Bretta is fearful of wearing the same outfit multiple times because it might end up on Facebook, Instagram, Twitter, or all three! However, it hurts her heart not to wear something again that she loves. When she does repeat her outfits, she is always careful to wait at least three months.

Bretta knows that she needs to change her mind-set—buying a new dress every week costs between fifty and one hundred dollars per week, depending on the dress. She was thankful that she had already started to make some changes when she explored her happy-hour strategy, so she had started to wean herself from her addiction to other people's approval and started evaluating who Bretta was. Therefore, she was more open to evaluate her clothing strategy.

Bretta's best friend Dana has amazing taste, and she suggested that—similar to what Jordan was doing by buying staple ingredients and creating different and interesting meals— Bretta could mix and match the outfits that she already owned. This way Bretta would look different but spend less money. Dana told Bretta, "If Kate Middleton, the Duchess of Cambridge, could repeat an outfit, then you certainly can!"

Dana suggested that Bretta change things up with a different belt, purse, or shoes, or change the look by wearing a jacket or light button-down top. Dana also suggested that Bretta use *Glamour* for inspiration, because the magazine generally has great ideas to switch up an outfit from day to night that she could leverage as creative inspiration. Finally, Dana suggested Pinterest as another place to find ideas for creating new outfits.

As Dana was leaving Bretta's condo, she told her a secret: "People are way too busy thinking about themselves to even notice what you had on three days ago, let alone three weeks ago! Don't sweat the small stuff. And trust me, this is small stuff!"

FNPhenomenal Action Item

1. Take a survey of your closet with a stylish friend to see how you can mix and match your clothing to make the outfits look different. Play with ideas.
2. If you do repeat an outfit, wear it with confidence. Remember, it is highly likely that no one will notice.

Questions to Ask as You

Identify Your Clothing

Strategy

1. Do I have the proper clothing staples?
2. What accessories, shoes, jackets, and so on can I leverage to create different outfits without spending money?
3. Why do I care so much about what other people think?
4. Who is paying my bills?
5. What about Bretta do I most identify with?

Potential Weekly Savings

Potential Weekly Savings: $50–$100

Amount Saved per Week: _____
Annual Savings: _____ x 4 x 12 = _____

PLUS 03:
TAMING THE MANE

Amber loves to work out and focus on health, but she also likes to look nice. She spends a lot of money making sure her hair still looks good even though she works out so much. In fact, she goes to the salon weekly. Each visit to the salon costs her twenty-five dollars, which is admittedly inexpensive compared to what most people pay. Amber doesn't necessarily want to get her hair done every week; however, in order to get the twenty-five-dollar rate, she has to visit the salon weekly. She actually knows how to do her own hair, but she's so convinced that twenty-five dollars a week is a great deal that she's been going weekly. Yes, she is guilty of spending money to save money.

As Amber started along this savings journey, she assessed this expense. "Is this expense really worth it?" she asked herself. Her response was no. As she started to think about her goals to develop a just-in-case fund and eventually start to pay off her credit card debt, she thought to herself, "A hundred dollars a month just isn't in my budget. It just isn't worth it to me. But I can't go to zero, so I will gradually scale back."

After this realization, Amber got back to doing her own hair. Her initial thoughts of "I can't live without my weekly Saturday routine" turned into "How hard is it to do my own hair, really?" She knew that she was not going to start coloring, trimming, or relaxing her hair, but she could do the easy stuff, like washing and straightening. As Amber started to think more about this step, she discovered another upside: it takes the same amount of time, if not less, to do her hair herself, because she *always* had to sit under the dryer forever when her stylist was double-booked.

When Amber told her friends what she was going to do, many of them discouraged her. However, Amber followed through with her plan. She moved from weekly to biweekly visits, and eventually from biweekly to monthly. She told herself that if she didn't shrivel up like the Wicked Witch in *The Wizard of Oz*, she would stretch going to the salon to whenever she needed her hair cut and layered. Once she realized how much money she could save and how beautiful her natural hair was, she traded that weekly cost for one bottle of eight-dollar shampoo and another of eight-dollar conditioner! Given how long bottled shampoo and conditioner last, she's saving a ton.

FNPhenomenal Action Item

1. Pick a day that you will wash your hair.
2. Wash, blow-dry, and flat-iron your hair. Also, try going natural.
3. If you don't know what to do, plenty of YouTube channels are available to teach you. Alternatively, pay attention to what your stylist does the next time you get your hair done, or ask a stylish friend for recommendations and tips.

Questions to Ask as You Identify Your Hair Strategy

1. Which days work best to do my hair?
2. How can I develop a routine that works?
3. Which products will I use?
4. Do I have everything I need?
5. What about Amber do I most identify with?

Potential Weekly Savings

Potential Weekly Savings: $25

Amount Saved per Week: _____
Annual Savings: _____ x 4 x 12 = _____

PLUS 04:
ONLINE SHOPPING AND "MUST-HAVE" DEALS

Nina loves her e-mail alerts for sales. She is a sucker for a good sale. Every time a new "Buy Now! Today Only!" e-mail comes out, Nina is in the store or online trying to "save money." One day Jordan asked her, "Have you ever noticed that the same sales pop up from week to week? That's because there is always a sale! The sales never go away!" At that point, Nina realized "limited time only" is not true all the time.

Nina thought about what she needed to do to control her urge to shop and to minimize temptation. This included unsubscribing from sale notification e-mail lists, deleting any shopping apps on her mobile phone, and removing her credit card from her account profiles to reduce the ease of shopping.

Nina knew that she didn't have the discipline yet to just say no. Therefore, she decided to stay away from anything that would tempt her—like the mall, e-mail notifications, and shopping apps—until she developed the discipline to just say no.

FNPhenomenal Action Item

1. Monitor your spending in this area for a week.
2. After a week, if you find that you are shopping via your apps or spending because you saw an e-mail, unsubscribe to e-mail lists and delete your smartphone shopping apps.

Questions to Ask as You Identify Your Shopping Strategy

1. What is the trigger that causes me to spend money? Is it the fear of a loss of a good deal? Is it the feeling of "needing" the item? Do I feel like I am missing that item in my closet? Is it something else?
2. When do I typically shop? Can it be attributed to boredom, emotional woes, or similar triggers?
3. Where do I typically shop? Is it in the mall, on the Internet, or via apps?
4. How can I combat the need to buy?
5. What about Nina do I most identify with?

Potential Weekly Savings

Potential Weekly Savings: Varies per person

Amount Saved per Week: _____

Annual Savings: _____ x 4 x 12 = _____

REFLECTION PAGE

PLUS 05:
ENJOY A WEEKLY STAYCATION

Jordan is always on the go. As she started her journey to financial freedom, she realized just how much her schedule affected her finances. She loves the daily hustle and bustle and filling up her schedule with an endless array of work, meetings, events, friend time, and playtime. She couldn't imagine things any other way. But she had to admit that it was exhausting, physically and financially.

Jordan realized that her fast pace is not sustainable. She's not the Energizer Bunny; she can't keep going and going and going. Jordan wasn't eating balanced meals or sleeping enough. Her brain was always turned all the way up. She'd crashed before and spent days recovering from being sick. Jordan started to understand the need for rest and relaxation, and not just because slowing her pace could help her financially. It could also help her physically. She once heard the saying, "Many people spend their youth sacrificing their health for wealth, but when they get older, they sacrifice their wealth to get their health back."

No amount of money or fun is worth sacrificing one's health. Jordan now understands that taking time to relax and take care of herself is priceless, because she is in life for the long run. Therefore, she committed herself to gaining greater control over her schedule and staying home once a week to relax and just do something simple that she would enjoy.

Merriam-Webster defines a staycation as "a vacation spent at home or nearby."

FNPhenomenal Action Item

1. Enjoy a mini staycation once a week.
2. Take this time to totally check out and relax. This not only allows you to save money (because you won't be at an event or a party or happy hour), but it also allows you to refocus your energy, relax, and concentrate on you and what you love. Spending time alone allows you to rebuild your strength and sanity. Trust me, your healthy future self will thank you.

Questions to Ask as You
Identify Your Staycation
Strategy

1. If I stayed home, what would I do?
2. How do I feel when I am always on the go?
3. What drives me to be on the move?
4. Do I wish I could spend more time alone?
5. What aspects of my life suffer when I am always running around?
   a. Do I sacrifice working out, eating right, or anything else related to my health?
   b. Am I spending enough time with my family and those who mean the most to me.
   c. Am I doing the things that help make me unique?
6. What about Jordan do I most identify with?

Potential Weekly Savings

Potential Weekly Savings: Priceless

Amount Saved per Week: _____
Annual Savings: _____ x 4 x 12 = _____

REFLECTION PAGE

AFTER THE TRIP

A year has passed since Nina, Bretta, Amber, and Jordan began their FNPhenomenal journey. As soon as they got back from their trip to Costa Rica, Nina, Amber, and Bretta got together for a girls' night at Jordan's condo, and they filled Jordan in on what she'd missed. They reminisced about touring a volcano, relaxing in a hot spring, trekking through the rain forest, going zip lining, and snorkeling in the gorgeous ocean. It was a true trip of a lifetime, and they can't wait to go back. Of course Jordan was sick with the thought of missing all of that!

As they continued to chat, they reflected on their yearlong FNPhenomenal journey and what they'd learned. The girls recognized that it wasn't easy at first. In fact, it took them about nine and a half weeks to develop the habit of using the identified money-saving strategies. After that time, the changes were ingrained. When times got tough, they reminded themselves why they were making the change. The three biggest hurdles that they had to overcome were the following:

1. **Preparation:** Sometimes they didn't feel like going to the grocery store or spending the time to make lunch, dinner, and so on. However, by preparing ahead of time, they maximized the likelihood of adhering to the plan.
2. **Daring to be different:** Even when their friends laughed at their new lives or didn't support them, Nina, Jordan, Amber, and Bretta supported each other and focused on why they were making the changes. They knew that the status quo was not an option, and they understood that change could be uncomfortable. Creating this support system made things a little easier.
3. **Fear:** The unknown can be scary. Unsure that they could stick with the plan and ultimately save money, they feared they would fail. However, they kept going anyway.

> **Focus on why you are making the change, as that will help carry you through the difficult times.**

After the year of saving, they had accomplished the following:

- Nina saved $2,500 over the course of the year: $600 by reducing online shopping, $400 by implementing the coffee swap, and $1,500 by bringing lunch. She didn't save the entire $1,800 because she slipped up a few times and bought lunch. However, she still saved over $2,000 because she reduced her online shopping more than expected. Since the Costa Rica trip cost $2,000, Nina used the balance to start an emergency savings account.

- Jordan saved $2,850 over the course of the year: $2,250 by making her own dinner, $100 by reducing the frequency of her manicures, and $750 by taking staycations. Since Jordan didn't go to Costa Rica, she split the savings between starting an investment account and repaying student loans.

- Amber saved $3,320 over the course of the year: $1,650 by bringing her lunch, $1,170 by changing her bottled-water strategy, and $500 by doing her own hair. Amber used $2,000 for Costa Rica and $500 to fund a just-in-case account. Since she saved more than she'd planned, she added a goal and put the remaining $820 toward credit card repayment.

- Bretta saved $4,200 over the course of the year: $1,500 by making her own lunch, $1,500 by reducing her visits to happy hour, and $1,200 by buying fewer party dresses. Though she was proud of her savings, she learned something more valuable: the importance of learning to be alone, serving the community, and learning who she was as a person. Nina, Amber, and Jordan were so inspired by

Bretta's new passion and outlook that they occasionally volunteered with her. After paying for the trip to Cota Rica, Bretta donated 30 percent of her remaining $2,200 to the charity organization where she volunteered, and put 70 percent toward credit card debt repayment.

Seeing that Nina, Jordan, Amber, and Bretta were so successful at saving their money without killing their lifestyles, some of their other friends and coworkers are now asking them for advice. And Nina, Bretta, Jordan, and Amber give advice freely, because they love helping other women become FNPhenomenal.

All of them are looking forward to next year's seven-day trip to Australia. Even Jordan is going to attend! The girls are going to become even more aggressive with saving this year now that they have other goals, including investments, emergency savings, just-in-case accounts, student loan repayment, and credit card debt repayment. Armed with their new FNPhenomenal habits and this information, they cannot wait until this time next year to reflect on how far they have come. Let the new savings goals begin!

EPILOGUE

Two of the biggest barriers to getting started are: 1) not knowing where to start, and 2) and feeling overwhelmed.

I'm a big fan of starting off small, with manageable steps, and working up from there. This guide was designed so you can pick a few things to save at least a hundred dollars a week, just like Nina, Jordan, Amber, and Bretta. Of course, if you are an overachiever, you can always do more!

Alternatively, if you need to start off with even smaller steps in order to stick to the strategies, then do that. If something isn't working for you, stop it and ramp up in another area. It's all about trial and error. Whatever you choose, try to follow the path in this guide for thirty days.

Move at your own pace. Trial and error is okay until you determine the strategy that works best for you. The important thing is that you start!

Whatever you do, do *something*. Doing nothing is not an option. The status quo isn't working. We often hear that the definition of insanity is "doing the same thing over and over again and expecting different results." Tell yourself that the status quo is not an option, and commit to change today.

Make a decision, and watch your life change. Sometimes it seems like the initial steps don't matter. However, Shirley Hufstedler, former US secretary of education, said it best: "You don't make progress by standing on the sidelines, whimpering and complaining. You make progress by implementing ideas." Get off the sidelines of financial freedom, and start putting your thoughts into action.

I'm not going to promise you that it will be easy. It won't. However, I will promise you that the reward is amazing. Knowing that you mastered something difficult and gained greater discipline and control over your life is worth it. Learning that your worth is determined not by how you spend your money but by who you are as a person is a powerful lesson. You need to take the first step, which is putting the tips in this FNPhenomenal guide to use. Once you master these, you will be well on your way to realizing the FNPhenomenal potential in you.

Be phenomenal!

♥ Aisha

www.ingramcontent.com/pod-product-compliance
Lightning Source LLC
Chambersburg PA
CBHW061049090426

42740CB00002B/86